MW01489425

BLUE STONE RING

BY:JOHN WESLEY BURTON

BLUE STONE RING

BY:JOHN WESLEY BURTON

Copyright © 2022 John W. Burton
1st Edition

All rights reserved. Reproduction and distribution of this work without
written permission is prohibited

ISBN: 9798355200589

A Burton Media Group Book
Burton Media Group, Morehead, Ky

Contents

The Blue Stone Ring

Summer breezes past
The Blue Stone Ring
Upon Blackbird Mountain
As a storm whirled passed
It is much more than just
A Blue Stone Ring
Upon Blackbird Mountain
She beholds her arch of bloom
As if its love and kindness
Was just as beautiful
As were her Blue Stone Ring
Listen to her and love
Her triumphant ring
Its stone the most
Beautiful blue
The same
As the Wild Blue Rose
The Blackbird Mountain
Guards her
The Forest Queen
The most modest
Gem of earth
Sweet blooming
The trembler fell
Timid the Blue Stone Ring
Knows the location
Of the mountain
That no one can find
It is the Blackbird Mountain

Standing Tall With The Blue Stone Ring

Fire Cracker Dan
Has a lot of kin
He can dance the dance
Of a thousand soldiers
Dancing in a marching band
There are more than
Three billion Blue Stone Rings
Out there somewhere
In this world
Fire Cracker Dan says
I know only one
Blue Stone Ring
And I am standing tall with her
If you ever find the magic
Of the Blue Stone Ring
Then you will have only
A slight chance
Of finding the Blackbird Mountain
First you still have to find
The crystal ball
And look through it
To see the Blue Stone Ring
The search
For the Blackbird Mountain
Continues soon

Weezer

He is a coon dog. The color of coffee
and cream. He is the greatest sniffer
of them all and the sharpest on the trail.
He is a friend of the little coons. He has
been searching for the Blackbird Mountain
for twenty-four years.

The Big Coon

He searched for the Blackbird Mountain
for the past twenty-four years. His favorite
food to eat is corn. His best friend is Weezer.

Bluetick

He is the Dog of Thunder. He was a guide to assist Weezer and the Big Coon to find the Blackbird Mountain.

Weeper

She is the Alien Calico Cat that
was to be a guide to assist Weezer and
the Big Coon with the searching and the
finding the Blackbird Mountain.

Dreaming About Tomorrow

Tomorrow holds more promise
Than it does today
There is more adventure
More hope of getting things done
Just before the curtain
Of time closes
Tomorrow has a way
Of disappearing
Don't fail to realize
That today
Will become yesterday
When tomorrow returns again
We need to keep track
Of our number of days
And apply our own wisdom
In our own use of time
We are alike
We dream of the future
For what is yet to come

The Musical Song

A Raven and a Blackbird
Met on a cliff upon
Blackbird Mountain
Each one could become
The King of Birds
The Turtle Fiddler
Played for them
A beautiful song
The two birds
Were touched
By his beautiful music
The Turtle Fiddler
Said
My friends
I play this song
For every Raven
And every Blackbird
That comes to this cliff
Upon my homeland
The Blackbird Mountain
The musical sounds
Are telling
Them a message
That they could
Deliver
To the campfire site
And tell it to
Weezer and the Big Coon
The Calico Cat
Weeper
Already knows
The message
Of the Turtle Fiddler's
Musical song
Let us not forget
That the Bluetick
The Dog of Thunder
Is still there

At the campsite
Could the Turtle Fiddler's
Musical song
Be telling them
Something about
The Crystal Ball
Remember if they find
The Crystal Ball
They have a chance
To find the Blue Stone Ring
Their search
For the Blackbird Mountain
Or the Mountain of Gold
Will come to an end

A Blue Stone Will Do

Little I ask my wants are few
I only wish a hut of stone
A very Blue Stone will do
That I may call my own
And close at hand is such a one
In yonder street that fronts the sun

Treasure on an Island

Shine forth the stars
Of poets with rage
Reading their poems
From a stage
Take flight into the night
When the Blue Stone Ring is at rest
When brass and copper fade
Look at all the ages from history
Measure the distance of time
All is well winter will return
Travel to the Blackbird Mountain
You may find a fortune
Waiting for you there
It could be the vacation
That you have never taken
You have traveled above your youth
Look through your binoculars
You will see
The wonders out there
You will become partaken
Within your happiness
The writer knows best
Fire that is the closest
Is the warmest fire
You can now see the treasure
On the mountain floor
The island is far away
Says the studious university
It was known that travels
You had none during your youth
How now
What poem will you read
On the stage today

Traveling of Time

Every time that I walked down
The tree-lined mountain
I would pray
That we would meet again
A glance of seeing you
Would bring back memories
From our old homestead
The torture of yesterday's dreams
Would rise to where you would know
That the passing of time
Had not taught me to forget you
I took a good look
At the secrets
Of how fast time travels
From seconds
To minutes
To days
To months
To years
Time is continuing
To travel with me
Through my continued
journey unseen

There Stood Only One

Bright is the Blue Star
The spirits closed their eyes to rest
Upon the Blackbird Mountain
There stood only one
With a blue flower-bud pure and rare
It wore a little robe of white
Free from all of the other arts
She gave her spirit to a hand
That led her out of the storm

The Writing

Extensive essays
Not at all of equal merit
Within many writings
There is acute logic
Nevertheless characterized
By its style
Which can be distinguished
By the listening to the music
Played by the organ
Always take a good look
At the writing
Of the political movement
Everything Goes Away
Olden time voices
I can still
Hear them from the distant past
They are as beautiful
As the happiest dreams
And they are as beautiful
As the Blue Stone Ring
The stream as she flows
Their faces I see them again
As they smile at the clouds
Flying through the sky
Deep waves from the sea
Sweeps the sand away
From its shores
Those olden memories
Are fading away
Within the beam of the sun
Just like the flowers
In the distance dies

Poems are Songs

All poems are songs
Poetry guides
Musical thoughts
Read deep enough
You will see musically
That the heart of Nature
Is music
If you can reach it
Music adds
To the power of good
We all can hear
The music is coming from
The Blackbird Mountain

Arrows

The archer's arrows
Of the Blackbird Mountain Pines
Gray shadows haunting
The ghosts
Upon the mountain
The sunshine is not
Shinning on the mountain
Today as they sleep
The wind sings
As the sky changes
From purple to blue
Mountain friends
Are the spirits blend
The ghosts speak
The language of the voices
Of the pines
A fir tree falls
To leave another behind
The lake is blue
Among wild wood flowers
Ghostly shadows blend
Within the mountain of fog
There is no fear
Upon the Blackbird Mountain today
The pines standing still
Their ghosts will never die
Far away and strange
Are the ghosts
Upon the Mountain of Gold
It is only ghostly
Shadows of dreams
Listen closely
Hear the crickets wailing
There she is the pale ghost
Of the setting moon
The Archer
Her arrows made
From the Blackbird Mountain pines

She paints the blue
In the sky
With the arrows
Released from her bow
The rising moon shines
On the hills
For the fonder dreams
The purple mountains
She witnessed throughout
The day
Now she watches
The silence of the night
With a strong embrace
Of the Blackbird Mountain
With many ghostly
Spirits upon her face

Song of Fallen Water

Her blue eyes
Have left all of us
The Spring-Birds
Have flown away
Look up yonder
Upon the Blackbird Mountain
There you will see
The pathway
Of the spirits
The hummingbird
Lives on our sacred land
We see this bird
Often from time to time
O spirit
Of the beautiful blue water
The canoe is upon
Your waves
The finest furs
Hang over her grave
Remember the robes
That she wore
We see her
Robes no more
Now a strange
Land she walks
It burns with sunshine
And it freezes with cold
Let us give
To the lost ones
The robes that she wore
We see the lost ones
No more
The path she now treads
Will soon be our own
We will be gliding
Within her shadow
Unseen tagging along
There will be the calling

Of souls gone before her
You will hear them
No more
There is a wigwam
Within the sunset
Shining through curtains
Of gold
We see her home
The wigwam
No more
There they are
The children
Of the fallen leaves
Down at the blue river
Where the high winds
And their voices
Are being born and dying
Nature's wild music
Can be heard down there
The birds are screaming
In the wailing
Of the breezes
It was her farewell song

Traveling Home (Battles No More)

One turns away
His mighty hands
The hopelessness
Repeating
All through life
He had nothing
In common
With his own living
He didn't spring
To leap
Towards the throne
He was all alone
Throughout the ages
His character
Never formed
He had faith
Within the common ranks
Of his powerful
Army of soldiers
Don't we all
Have flaws which vein
The blue marble
Of our character
Many times he began
Drifting through
Which his divine
Purpose had been Achieved
He understood
Not the journey
For someday he will
Be at home
The place
Where his battles
Will be no more

Dream the Dream of Dreams

A sleeps long night
It had been
Only a dream it was
A dry forest
The desert became
All gone were the trees
Not a cloud in the sky
Several summers now
Brown grass never
Green again
No more
The motor car
On the water
The ocean you
Will be walking
Dream the Dream
Of Dreams
Touching the sky
The mountains where
The wild bear
Was running
Deadly winds
Amongst them
Dream the Dream
Of Dreams
There you knew
You were
Beyond the milky way
Within the universe
Real was his Dream of Dreams
They were the finding
Of the Blackbird Mountain

Brave Warrior

The whole subject
Was the loss
Lightning-struck
The array of numbers
Of the soldiers in battle
The castle rises
Quickly out of the deep
And happy fields
Look upon him
The one who brings
To you the place and time
We called the pitchy cloud
Riding with the eastern wind

Traveling Home

Dream not
Of their flight
Our great
Expectations
It should
Be called
Nor can this be
It wasn't their
Legal work
The stars shall
Return every night
The prince of air
Became the light
Of darkness
The enemies of truth
His warriors will defend
They are not afraid
The wolves will succeed
While their own
Advantages will turn
Towards rites
And specious forms
The world will
Continue to move forward
We all are in the race
Of time
There is no ending
Of where your
Blue eyes can't reach
We will depart
Through our
Peace of thought
Accomplishing
Great things
Which are deemed
As being weak
Death comes through
The gate of life

I say of
All the riches
Of this world
Who am I
During the next
Many days
My thoughts
Will become
Unanimously sad
Someday there will be
A happy ending

Life of Everyday

The dew that laid
On the ground
Was gone
The wilderness
Had a small face
They wished not
What it was
It is the food
Upon the ground
That has been
Given to you
To eat

The Other Soldiers

The prospect of war
Everyday increased
A short period
Of fighting elapsed
One must succeed
In taking some
Influential soldier
Keeping him prisoner
Of war
An officer
Of the other army
Passed through
The village
Just before dusk
In the late afternoon
It was a fine
Moon light night
They quietly
Marked the glittering
Of its beams
Within the polished arms
Of the other soldiers
This was the moment
In which
We were entertained
By the apprehension
Of war

The Eagle

Beautiful woven
Together traditions
Measure of the flow
Hoof-beats
Of the horses
Tremendous thunder
Upon Blackbird Mountain
Paddle strokes
Of the great ship
School crafts
Were found in books
The fox lives
In the wild woods
Gray smoke
From the fire
Curled above the river
As thunder remained
Upon Blackbird Mountain
The bird's nest
In the cliffs and trees
In the forest
Belongs to the eagle
The valley
Within the forest floor
Was silent
But the pine-trees
Were singing
There were no tribes
Of men there
Always love the shadow
Of the forest
Whether it be
A calm rain storm
Or a tornado
Voices of nature
Were from far away
Darkness came
Like that of the helpless

Blind just outside
Of the neglected
Graveyard with tombstones
Gray covered with moss
Footsteps flowed
Like the running
Of water in large rivers
Within the flame
Of a small burning fire
There was a signal
Warning directed
To all nations
Tree limbs
Were like the magical
Wand of the Red Oak tree
The warrior is the water
That travels
Upon the desert floor
Where were the war weapons
That were painted
The colors of the leaves
Of a maple tree
In late Autumn
There is always
A thrust of vengeance
And quarrels
Among nature
The Eagles are singing
The song of wisdom
And the song of warning
Why hurt one another
The wars
Will be of prayers
For revenge
How will they prosper
Through battle
The warriors
Came from the river
They were silent
But did not bury

Their weapons
There was a great bear
Of the Blackbird Mountain
This monster was one
That you must see
The war-club
The war-cry
The great bear
Of the Blackbird Mountain
Trembled
And whimpered
Like that of a coward
It had been conquered
In battle
And went into
Hiding upon
Blackbird Mountain
When the bear
Went into hiding
So did the nations
Of all of the world
From the bow
Came silver arrows
The forest was sleeping
Frogs were singing
On the river banks
From the river
Came the most
Beautiful music
The sun was smiling
Above the smoldering
Fire that burned
No more
It was a miracle
The fire without fuel
Started to burn
Bright and smoke again
The last rose
Is now defeated
It had wrestled

With the enemy
Until it became
Feeble and staggering
To the ground
It was the eagle
That saw
The wild-goose
And the ripe
Clusters of blue grapes
When the river
Water twinkles
Amongst the yellow trees
The war will be over

A Soldiers Weapon of Words

The other half
Of the journey
Is yet to come
Feast with me
At my journey's end
To answer any question
I must stand again
Endeavour my deeds
To match my words
Beat loud the tambourines
And let the trumpets blow
The musical sounds
Played by other soldiers
That I used to know
The surgeon's box
Was on the patient grounds
I feared no bear
I went on to speak
A grain a day
I would not buy
Courage was all
I could have given
I knew my drift
Which a soldier
Should bare
When the sea was calm
All the boats were calm
Like lonely dragons
Floating on the water
I talked of more
Than I have seen
Bid me farewell
With a smile
The enemy is gone
I have spoken
Using my weapon
Of words

The Location of Blackbird Mountain

Blackbird Mountain
Is a distant mile
From another land
Unknown
Within two trees
That stand by a river
A mile from another mountain
There are only
Two roads going through
This mountain
In different directions
It is covered with a forest
Belted with fertile ground
Its height rises
To thousands of feet
You can see this mountain
From a distance
Of fifty miles away
Weezer and the Big Coon
For more than
Twenty-four years
Shadowed the miles
That they had traveled searching
For Blackbird Mountain
With no discovery
If they were to return
To the beginning
Of their search
They would have no
Memory of the years
Of searching and not finding
The Mountain of Gold

A Diamond or Coal

A diamond if you please
Who cares about
A block of coal
Beneath the summer trees
A diamond or coal
Coal if you please
Out comes to care
About the coal
At times
When water freezes

What is it

In marble walls
White as milk
Lined with a skin
As soft as silk
Within a fountain
Crystal clear
A golden apple
Does appear
No doors
Are to this threshold
Yet thieves break in
And steal the gold

Blackbird Mountain's (Fairy Queen)

It is hard to always
Be anybody's enemy
For the Fairy Queen
Lives upon
Blackbird Mountain
Into her yearning
Blue eyes were filled
With happy tears
What trouble
Is within her final while
Has the watchful
Man in the tower
Become old and gray
Was it a bitter war
Hope is never dead
The dreadful darkness
Of all things
Living shuns

Building a Railroad

If willing to do so
We all can learn
To build a railroad
The building
Of a railroad
Can be any job
That people
Are working at
Throughout
My working years
I have seen
Many people working
High level jobs
Who actually
Could not build
A railroad
No one can
Build anything
If they don't work
To get any job done
The correct way
Even today
We all should be
Building a Railroad

The Forest of the Night

In what distance
Ground or sky
Burnt the fire
Of thine eyes
On what wings
Dare he aspire
Thy hand seized
The fire
The stars threw
Down their spears
And watered heaven
With their tears
Everything was burning
Bright in the forest
Of the night

A Lonely Place

The rain had fallen
A light wind
Blew from the gates
Of the sun
He sat down
In a lonely place
The wild-swans
Paused and looked
Up at the clouds
In the sky
The bluebirds
Stopped hunting
For the bees
The snake
Held her own
While a wild hawk
Was standing
On her ground
Looking at his prey
The snake had sung
Many songs
Today she sings
A song of what the world
Will become
After the years
She had died
And went away

A Rented Room

It didn't matter who he was
He rented the cheapest
Room that I had
He had the right
As anyone of being there
We met on the street once
The wind turned his head
The other way
He didn't speak to me
We met on the stairs
The sound of a train
Turned his head
The other way
He didn't speak to me
Once we met
Outside his door
He turned his head
The other way
He didn't speak to me
He had the right
To do as he pleased
I know who rents
My rooms
I don't like any renter
Of my rooms
Never having nothing
To say to me
He paid his rent
A week in advance
I wonder
Will he turn his head
Another way
Will he speak to me
When I tell him
That it is time
For him to go
And I told him
That I would never

Rent a room to him again
Did he ever speak
To her or did he turn
His head the other way

On My Doorstep

I knew the storms of tears
Which rained kindness
Upon my broken heart
I knew the hostility of fear
Not long-ago happiness
Stood on my doorstep
There it was again today
I opened my door
To the return of happiness
And I told her to never
Leave my home again

Pity and Kindness

Pity has no room
In the house of Kindness
Poverty is only gloom
Of pity at its best
The House of Kindness
Puts them both to rest
Don't regard objects
Fallen by the way
Of kindness and love
We don't seek
For we are strong
We leave them
To the poor and meek
Where should they be
Poverty and pity
They must travel
With a bow and arrow
To the ages
Of power and wealth
Poverty and pity
We must not see or hear
Of them anymore
Kindness and love
Must live
Inside of your doors

Essence of a Dream

I am writing with my pen
Within the honeyed
Meaning of a dream
You could pick
Me an apple from
The tallest apple tree
I will not come to dance
You can see my thoughts
Like you can sing the notes
Sung by a small bird
In a cloak of dreams
I see the stars
You don't have to run
To spread your fears
It is only the honeyed
Essence within a dream

Stock Market Crash of Twenty-Nine

Think of those
Childhood days
The wolf of take
Was outside
Of their doors
For others
Desires of want
Drowned before
Their eyes
One child
Saw a frail of desire
That his life
Had failed to drown
His playing a fiddle
In the street
One morning
He whimpered toons
That he knew
A poor lady
Walked up to him
And gave him a dime
It was the whining
Of the fiddler's plea
It was given
To him for only
The realm of sound
He became a wizard
At playing the fiddle
It was the fall
Of the stock market
Twenty-Nine
He clapped
His aching hands
His final note had died
He thought back
To his tin of coffee
And his bowl of soup
All that he wanted in life

Was to survive
The Great Depression
The stock market
Crash of Twenty-Nine

Blue Stone Roses

The roses I have given
To her today
Were Blue Stone Roses
With the fragrances
Of kindness and happiness
She said you bought
These roses for me
They were as colorful
As any beautiful blue
Flower could be

The Tumble Weed

The summer sun
Hot as she shuns
Upon what is now
The desert floor
Finally after months
Of dry skies
Clouds and wind
Are with me today
I watched
As the tumble weed
Rolled by
As if I wasn't there
Drought has taken
The crops
Nothing grows
In hard baked soil
The tumble weed did
Roll by me today
Sure sign of rain
It was just about noon
There were clouds
And wind
But still no rain
The crops growing
In this desert have died
Several days ago
The tumble weed
Still rolling
Being moved by
The waterless wind
It was a gray sky
That was as dry
As the desert floor
The tumble weed
Was out of sight
The wind blew
As dry as she was
The clouds were nothing

But desert drought
When will
The tumble weed
Return to the desert
And see me
Planting another crop
There is no need
How can one eat
When he sees
Only the return
Of the tumble weed
The sky is gray
Again today
The wind is moving
Dust thoroughly
Throughout
The land of no trees
Will I see her again
The tumble weed
There now is no
Water to drink
For the desert
Spring has become
Dried mud
It is cloudy
Again today
The land
That was covered
With beautiful green grass
Is it so dry
That it would
Set a blaze
From only one
Spark of flame
The tumble weed
Returned today
The sun
Talked to the clouds
And the wind
And said

The tumble weed
Must return
Here another time

The Bridge

Once there lived
Two Turtle Fiddlers
Upon Blackbird Mountain
They knew
The ancient master
A man of knowledge
After many suns had gone
He swore not to wear
Another man's shoes
Maybe he will wear
Another man's shoes
Who understands him
Better than I do
Two mules were
The builders of the bridge
One mule says
To the other mule
Remember that it was we
Who carried the stones
But man claims
He built the bridge
All by himself
Before the building
Of the bridge
There was a wild river
To cross
The water became
An unknown road
To the swimmer wrestling
With the rushing waters

Dreaming of Gold

I walked through
The Blackbird Mountain
In my dream of gold
It was far too much
For my hands to hold
Gold was glittering
Upon the yellow sea
The whole mountain
Became a Liberty Bell
Of gold
Golden was the dirt
And golden was the sun
Both became as one
Be safe within
The golden rhythm
And free the dreaming
Golden images of time

Shaking the Apples Down from the Tree

The day before
I became a soldier
And went away from
My mountain home
My mother scarcely
Said a word
Then she said
It is such
A beautiful day
Let us go and shake
Some apples
From the apple tree
Time does move
Quickly
Twenty years
Had flown by
Since mother and I
Stood beneath
A shower of apples
Falling from our shaking
Of the apple tree
Her memory is fading
Away now
She said to her boy
The soldier of war
Your hands are still small
Just like they were
When we were together
Shaking apples
Down from the apple tree

Stole Dat Chicken

Yer say
I stole dat chicken
I preach down in Macon
And neber
Libs on luxuries
Cep cabbage and bacon

The Crossroads

Where was beauty
And ugly traveling
On the Crossroads
Their tales
Came from the dust
Swirling like a whirlwind
Will beauty and ugly
Someday meet
On the Crossroads
Beauty and ugly
Always travels
In different directions
Beauty is the summer sun
And ugly is the whirling
Of the twisting
Funnel shaped cloud
Touching the ground
Riding with the wind

The Swimmer

Even though
You can't swim
Wear your life jacket
And don't dive
Into a body of
Water that is over
You head

Can't Have It All

I don't know
It is hard to explain
When you are living
Well above your means
You have so much debt
That you will never
See daylight
The road if tougher
Than people think
You can make a lot
Of money
Think about earning
All of that money
Working from
Day to day
That becomes
Years to years
Don't forget your debt
You will make
A lot of money
Working
Your entire lifetime
After all is said
And done
Have you counted
Your money
You were paid
Throughout your lifetime
Of work
Did you count
Your money
That you have given
To other folks
Throughout your lifetime
Of work
As your days of work
Went forward
And become years

When your first day
Of work
Had been completed
You were young
But look at you now
You are old
And the other folks
Have lived well
Off of the money
You have given them
Throughout
Your lifetime of work
Your dream was to earn
Through your work during
Your lifetime
A lot of money for yourself
But the largest percentage
Of the time
It is for you to give
It away to someone else
I can write these words
Because
For days that became years
I had traveled
The road to work
From here to there
And from there back
To here
Look at me now
I am not
Young anymore
I am older than the hills
And broke
Because I gave all of my lifetime
Of working to someone else

Got It All

What if I had
All that I needed in life
There is no want
For anything else
Did I say
Got all I need in life
Let's say I have
More than I will
Ever need
I know that there
Is no way
That I can take it all
With me at my ending
Chapter of my life
There are many people living
Out there who doesn't
Have a clue of the value
Of anything
But those people
Who do are like me
They have everything
That they need in life
What does it mean
When you have it all
And have no need
For anything else
Maybe a person
Could have treasure
That used to be another
Persons so-called trash
A treasure is never trash
Some places
Especially Cracker-Barrel
Show cases their treasures
For their customers
To enjoy by looking
At them before
They order their meal

And after they pay the cashier
Some folks can
See the value
Of everything
Especially yesterday's
Treasures
The longer you keep
What you got
The more wealth
It would bring to someone
Someday
As long as there
Is high demand
For what you have collected
And hidden away for years
How can life be great
When a person
Has no need or want
For anything else
When his treasured
Collection
Has grown so large
It is time
To downsize
Get rid of it
To the degree
That I don't
Have it all
I will then have
Want and need
For something else

Broken Promises

She stood between
Two broken promises
There was a gray sky overhead
Looking down
At the City of the Living
Palaces were standing tenantless
Where were those
Who wore the crown
She continued to stand between
Two broken promises
Upon a sunlit scene she heard about
The Blackbird Mountain
The one she can't find
The sky seemed as it was one
Vast temple with walls
Of gold and blue
She saw an island
Floating on a wave
An island she wouldn't reach
There it is the bitter stream
She now stands on
The Land of Dreams
In her heart was a fallen city
A moment later she stands
Looking at the Isle of Dreams
The waves are playing
On the sand
Her standing is over
She now doesn't stand
Between two broken promises
Anymore

A Cloud in the Sky

I saw a beautiful cloud
In the sky this morning
It floated gently
Over the coming hour
I watched it rising
As it gently floated away
The cloud that I saw
In the sky this morning
I thought it resembled life
As it ushered out of this world

Beautiful Blue Eyes

The past was silent
Resting upon the distant sand
Climbing the high cliffs of time
The sound of church bells ringing
Thinking about the future
As Softly flowing the water goes
Have you not seen the frozen sails
The white-winged ocean birds
The lady with her beautiful
Blue eyes wearing
Her Blue Stone Ring of Power
Seeing her past widening visions ahead
The Blackbird Mountain
Vanishes in thin air
The past comes to life again
The present is never lost
Of what it is
To whisper is only the dreaming
Of the silent past
Just as the big rain drops fell
She has returned again
To the place where it all begin

One Heart

His heart was hardened
All prayed for him with tears
Hold your peace
There shall be none other-wise
The year was 1347
For he sailed sweeping
The narrow seas
With one heart
The people he ruled
The showiness of falsehood
Ran through his personal character
He paraded his mistress
His Queen of Beauty
Through the golden roads
Upon The Blackbird Mountain
He was the most prominent scholar
And was natural in his defense
Of independence
He had no quarrel
With the doctrines of Rome
In Ireland the spirits
Of the people
Were there

Only One Treasure

Somewhere within this world
there is only one treasure out
there that is more precious to
me than the largest diamond.

This Person

If you find someone
Who makes you smile
Who checks up on you
Often to see if you are okay
Who watches out for you
And wants
The very best for you
Don't let someone
like this go
Keep this person
Close because people
Like this are hard to find

The Voices of the Kentucky Children
Who is Fire Cracker Dan

Their poems they tell you who he is or what he can do for them.

Fire Cracker Dan is a stopper

He stops
Wrecks
Before
They happen
He stops
People
From taking
Something
From
Somebody
He stops
People
From hurting
Each other
He stops
People
From hurting
Themselves
With
Drugs and meth
Fire Cracker Dan
He is
The man
If he
Can't fix it
Nobody can

Fire Cracker Dan is A Superhero

Fire Cracker Dan
He is
The man
If he
Can't fix it
Nobody can

Fire Cracker Dan is a helper

He helps
People
With their work
He helps
Everybody
To get
Enough food
To eat
He helps
Everybody
To have
A good place
To call home

Fire Cracker Dan is a fixer

He fixes
My grandpa
So he won't
Have cancer
He fixes
My road
So the bus
Can get
Through ok
He fixes
Our room
At school
So we
Don't
Have to have
Buckets
For leaks

Fire Cracker Dan is a Maker of Better Things

He makes
Our school
Days shorter
He helps us
Like food
That we
Don't like
He helps us to
Pay attention
When a class
Is hard for us

Fire Cracker Dan says

There's no place like home
It doesn't matter
How far away you travel
you will always end
Up back home

I can walk away
From work tomorrow
Forever and live alone
Upon the Blackbird Mountain

Through all networking sites
Are there really any true friends
Out there on the communication highway
Is friend and follow just two words
that have been chosen
From the seven days of wonder
Which still exist upon
The mountain that nobody can find

There are no tears today
For all of the storm clouds
Have gone home

No other chicken
Tells this big chicken
How he should live his life
The big chicken takes
Some advice from other chickens
But he does what he has to do
To live his life his own way
I thought about this big bird

How well he had done
By living his own life
Without the other chickens
Telling him what to do

This bird worries a lot
It travels in both directions
at the same time

There are tears today
Falling from the sky
At Fire Cracker Dan Land
It is raining
In the scenic Red River Gorge
Within the mountains
Of the Daniel Boone National Forest
A lady living in Florida
Told me once
That she would trade
The water for the mountains
I guess if all you see
around you is water
The mountains would look
Extremely beautiful to you

She took the slow-moving train
And never parted from me again

Her beautiful blue eyes sparkled
As she looked at me
After all she is the beauty queen

A pleasing land
Of beautiful purple grass
It was of dreams
That were at times
Never there
Gray thunder coming
From the sky
Running the sun away
From the beautiful
Flower that you
Many years ago
Have not found me there
An old song written by

An old worshipful gentleman
He owned an expensive estate
The poor stood at his gate
His old study was filled full
Of old learned books
There he was the old
Reverend Chaplain
Many know him by his looks
With an old fishing pole
Without a hook
An old kitchen with too many
Women that couldn't cook

I would rather talk
To the Blue Stone Ring
As to talk to anyone else
In this world

If they hadn't drained the cooker
It would still have beans in it

Like snow-falls on a river
one moment white
then gone forever

My words are as powerful
As the finest diamond
And of the purest gold

How far that little candle
Throws its beam
So shines her good deed
In this world of yours
She does nothing
for herself

The seven days
Of wonder
I often thought
Is my name just

As cold as snow
When my face
Has been seen
He is not the
Greatest king
Keep in mind
It is only a thought
Resolve all doubt
There is always
Goodly arrays
Standing there
Is the scene
Of numbering events
A few yards
In the distance
All stands still
Upon their education
Improved within several
Particulars the more
Wit than we
If I get through
This scene
The benefit of mankind
Will become preserved
Little Venus
Attended and all
Had become improved
With every passing hour
Distemper is but a trifle
In hopes you
Smoke your letters
Before you deliver them
Thank about it clearly
Did you ever rob
A bird nest
Did you notice
How fearful it became
If they were to leave
Their nest
Seems as every bird moves

Following her is what
We call a beauty queen

The Storm

As I live through
The days of wonder
There is a storm
Upon Blackbird Mountain
Is it a different storm
Or is it the same storm
That I have seen
Up there many
times before
Storm of Wonder
The day was sunny
There was no wind
Blowing at all
Dark clouds
Begin to gather
Above my head
Wind rocking the trees
Upon the Blackbird Mountain
We know where
The rain comes from
The dark clouds
Think about it
Where did the raging wind
Come from
Does it always ride
With the storm of wonder

Scorpio

Scorpio is driven
By tremendous power
And extreme strength
Scorpio is the most
Intense Zodiac sign
Of them all
The word that defines
A Scorpio the best
Is independent
They don't rely
On anybody
For their work
They feel content
Working their own
Way through
The sun transits
This sign of the Zodiac
Is form October 23
To November 22
A Scorpio never shows
His cards
Scorpio has Mars
As its minor ruler
Mars is the God of War
Who is depicted
Of charging into battle
So there is where
War on My Door Step
Originated from
A Scorpio knows
All of your secrets
And can read
Your thoughts
As easy as he/she
Can read a children's book
They are always determined
And will see things
Through to the end

Their powerful ideas
And energy means
That they are capable
Of success

Climbing an Eastern Kentucky Mountain

Illustrations that accompanied
A textbook over
One hundred years ago
Were planned
To alert the mind
And at its very best
More than half
Of the battle of teaching
The difficulty
Of learning was reading
It is as uninteresting
As playing a piano
Any reading teacher
Then and now
Will tell you
That learning to read
Is like climbing
An Eastern Kentucky Mountain

Our World

This world
That we live in
To work
To lend
To spend
To give in
To beg
To borrow
Could there have
Been a better
World out there
Somewhere else
That was never
Known to us

Literature of Old
Shakespeare
Milton
Wordsworth
Burns
Tennyson
Bryant
The words
Of such men
Do not stale
Upon us
They do not
Grow old or cold
You are the young now
But someday day
You will be old
It requires the committing
To memory
The chosen passages
Of the great authors
The relish
Of higher literature
Belongs to a few

Poetry requires
Knowledge
Of the superior culture
According to yesterday's
Authors it is better
To learn from the writings
Of the old

The Deck of Cards

It is greater for anyone
To be better than bitter
Sometimes a person can
Keep what has been
dealt to her or him
But sometimes
You can exchange
The cards
Or hand that has been
Dealt to you
Everyone needs to travel
From a negative direction
To a positive outcome
You the better person
Can never be torn down
Any choice that you have
Will always belong to you
Remember you hold
The entire deck of cards

Morehead State University Governor Scholars Creative Writing Class Letter to Fire Cracker Dan Summer 2021 and 2022

Hamilton
GSP Morehead
26 Cardinal Ln.
Winchester, KY
40391

Please give
to John Burton
+ Fire Cracker Dan

Dear John —

Thanks again for a super program. The students loved it! You are so creative & talented! I hope you can come to writing camp sometime. Thanks so very much!

Jacqueline
the teacher

July 28, 2021

Dear John,

Thank you for taking time out of your morning to share your world with us. I feel honored to have met you and Fire Cracker Dan before he becomes too popular to remember me.

I appreciate your creativity and eagerness to gather an international community. After hearing from you, I have been interested in learning about the history of coal country in Kentucky. I also see the importance of listening to individuals' stories.

I wish you and Fire Cracker Dan and his next-of-kin much success. Maybe, one day, I'll find Blackbird Mountain myself and know that an answer exists after all.

Sincerely,

Elisabeth Kemprs
Governor's Scholars Program 2021
Creative Writing & Literary Studies

July 27th, 2022

Dear John,

Thank you so much for coming to talk to us about your writing and creations the other day. I loved listening to you talk about your poetry, and you're commitment to your work is truly inspiring. Most of all, my favorite part of our talk was when I got the learn about Firecracker Dan. Your creation is amazing, and I'm so glad I got a picture with it! Thank you for taking time out of your day to speak to us, you are appreciated.

Sincerely,
Heather Denny

7/29/22

Dear John,

   Thank you so much for sharing Firecracker Dan with us. He's such a fun character. I loved the mixer one the most. I also really liked the poetry that went with him. Thank you for taking time out of your day. You were really kind.

                              Sincerely,
                              Bethany

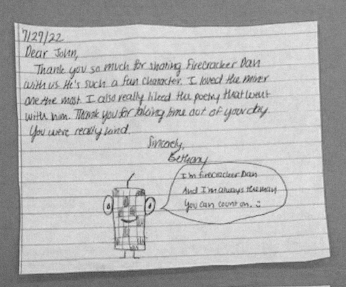

I'm Firecracker Dan
And I'm always the way
You can count on. :)

D7/27/2022

Dear John,

Thank you for letting us come in and talking to us about Firecracker Dan. I loved hearing about your writing process for your poems and how Firecracker Dan came to be. You're such a sweet and kind person, and I wish you nothing but good things in your future. Again, thank you!

Warm wishes,
Walline C. Palley

July 30th, 2021

Dear John,

Thank you so much for speaking with our Creative Writing Class here at the Governor's Scholars Program! I am a huge fan of Fire Cracker Dan! I especially loved the poem about modernizing nursery rhymes. Again, thank you for speaking with our creative writing class!

Best Regards,
Hannah Richards

Dear John,

Thank you so much for taking time to speak to us. Your introduction to Fire Cracker Dan (as I had never heard of him before) has made me feel closer to my inner Kentucky roots. But your introduction of your poetry books, like the one about the girl who got hypothermia in the mountains, was most impactful to me. Your bending of words to create such a vibrant story made me inspired to write my own poetry about things that I've heard and experienced. So thank you!

Sincerely,
Neha

7-28-21

Dear John,

Thank you so much for sharing your beautiful and hilarious poetry. I really enjoyed your passion for your work and fire cracker dan. It's very cool that you're created a whole movement with this character and have inspired many Kentuckians. Your charisma was very admirable and I was very entertained during our class period. You are one of the most memorable people I have met here on campus and I'll always remember the impact you're made. I'm a really big fan and I'm really glad I was able to meet fire cracker Dan and the man behind him.

Sincerely,
Khadijatol Jah

p.s. I think its really cool the richest man in the world made a mistake

Dear John,

7-28-2021

Thank you so much for speaking with our Creative Writing class about your writing and your stories. I loved reading your poetry and hearing about Fire Cracker Dan. It was also really cool to see your sketches and figures! Ya' were a lot of fun to talk with, and I can't wait to see what other stories and poetry you'll write.

Sincerely,

Kaylee Bliss

I was in Florida taking a two-hundred-ton boat ride on the Gulf of Mexico. The boat traveled swiftly among the waves just like the dolphins that came out to play. I have written over seven hundred poems. The question that I have to ask my Facebook Friends and everyone living throughout the geographical location of every particle of the sand--When should I allow my poetry writing to be blown away by the wind? Within this writing you don't hear or see any character known to all of us as Fire Cracker Dan. Will he also be blown away by the ocean's waves that creates the wind?

The Dolphins Came out to Play

Dolphins diving here and there
Over the waves without a care
Lazily gliding through the sea
Perfect animals so gentle and free
Happily they talk and play
In the water they frolic all day
Naturally beautiful and smart
Surely a wonderful work of art
Today the dolphins came out to play
I watched them jump for joy
From the two hundred ton vessel
That I was aboard going for the ride
With the cool wind leading the way
It seemed just then they were wise old men
And I a foolish girl
Atop the mighty waves they danced
To the rhythms of the moon
In harmony with the song of the sea
They played in perfect toon
Behind me fast cars rushed by
Towards some other time and place
What wonders do we never see
That stare us daily in the face
Today the dolphins came out to play
I never felt so small
And yet so grand
Bare feet in the sand
I love the sea
As well as I love the land

The Last Wildwood Flower

The last wildwood flower
Of summer
Blooming all alone
All of the others
Had faded and gone away
There is no other
Wildwood flower there
The pines are asleep
Wildwood flower
Go to sleep with them
The garden is silent now
Soon you will follow
You have no friends
With you today
The circle is shining
The rain drops
Have gone way
You will not inhabit
This world all alone
So wildwood flower
It won't be long
You will also
Fade and go away
Nothing is forever
Here to stay

Home

I couldn't admit
How far down I'd gone
How hopeless I felt
Faced with a step
Backwards
Into a wrong direction
What made
It more difficult
The whole town
Had changed
New stores and houses
Not a face
That I recognized
Much as I wanted
To come back home
Home wasn't
There anymore
I became ashamed
To meet my own blue eyes
I walked to the door
There it was
An awkward silence
Those confronting
Old bells
That I had
Completely forgotten
About
That reminded me
Of my home
That once was here
A home
Where I was always
Welcomed
Before the coming
Of that storm
A Little Cook Book
I am the lady
Who bought

This little cook book
My buying it
Tests its ware
I threw away all
Of my other cares
Tell your neighbor
Cooks to buy
Themselves
A copy of this
Little cook book

The Wildwood Flower

The Summer
Had come and gone
Just like a storm
That was visiting
Our Blackbird Mountain
I can say
That Fall of the year
There was none
This morning frost
Covered the ground
I don't have a clue
Of what was really
On my mind
As I was walking
Through a field
Of a hundred acres
Of brown plants
Just like the leaving
Of Summer
And no Fall
The storm I haven't
Seen one for
Some time now
I wanted to find
Only one
But the beautiful
Wildwood Flower herself
Was gone
A different one
Will be born
Some time next Spring
It seems to me
Like everything
Will be here
And then all
Will be gone
Even the Beautiful
Wildwood Flower

I use to know
Especially the one
Without a song

Different

Slow rises worth
By poverty depressed
Toil envy want
The patron
And the jail
The badge
Of the three
Holly leaves
With the motto
Sub sole sub
Umbra virens
Which are the arms
Of your family
It is like some
People of old
Have spoken
Of a cooled
Long age
In the
Deep-Deep earth
Such honors Lion
To her hero
She would pay
And peaceful slept
In the hot
Summer's Shade
I can't deem
That mother nature
Had done him
Any wrong
No chronic torches
Racked his age
The treasures
Of the deep
Are not so precious
As the scent
The smell
Of fresh air

Truth is a thing
That we all
Will forever keep
I think I
See an eagle
Bedazzling her eyes
At the full
Mid-day beam
While I'm looking
At the castled hall
The town was crowned
With shade
All that would desire
Could fly through
The earth
Look well beyond
The town
You will see
That of a flower
Deep and hidden
In a rocky cliff
Smile though
As if you are only
Looking at the sky
It is just
As the caterpillar
Had eaten
The leaves
Of this past spring's
Sweetest book

Who was Pocahontas

The daughter of Powhatan
A powerful Indian chief
From where is today
The Commonwealth
Of Virginia
He was born in 1595
She was captured
By the English
In 1612
And was held
As a safeguard
Against the hostility
Of her tribe
Plowed Ground
Standing upon the sweet
Smelling ground
There it is
The crystal blue sky
And the beautiful
Yellow landscape
Like a well-cooked steak
The richness of the ground
Showed her colors as well
The air was bitterly cold
Above the tall trees
That stood in the woods
The Earth and the sky
Remained silent that day
There were the lonely calls
Of the blackbirds upon
The Blackbird Mountain
The stream was running
Like the hands
On the face of a clock
The mules came out
To plow today
Their labor
Is for future hours

Not Long Now
There were the chains
Of darkness
With many troubles
Day and night
There was a shepherd boy
Who washes the sheep
The day will come
There will be feet
Walking on streets of gold
Work upon this Earth
Will come to an end
When time tells you
To rest
Fire will melt
This wicked world
If there is not a search
Within this world
Far and wide
And within the sea
So deep
There will never be
A finding peace

This World

Out in this cold world
And far away from home
A mother's child
Is wondering all alone
There is no one out there
To guide him
Or keep him traveling
In the right direction
My boy is homeless tonight
Mother will keep searching
Until she finds him
And will bring
Him back home
No matter how far
Away he may be
If you see him
Out there somewhere
Tell him that his mother
With her faded hair
Is at home
And she is waiting
For him there
Mama remembers
The parting words
That he had said
I am gladly
Going to close
My eyes
And then I will be
At rest
There is not another
That is left
To give me joy
Bring back to me
My wondering boy
We will meet again
At a place
Where no more

Tears will be shed
There will never
Be another good-bye
The new land
Will be so fair
Mother promised him
When I am done
With my life
Upon the Earth
I will meet you there
Upon this new land
Beautiful Indian Maid
The broken sword
A desperate fight
Stand-alone soldier
Throughout the wilderness
Roaming as a warrior
With bleeding wounds
Fighting still
There is a light
That shines
From the torch
Of death
Not to die by the fire
This soldier will not cry
Dances with
The savage crowd
A fearless heart
That will confront
The murderous blades
A beautiful Indian Maid
Daughter of a King
Indian fires
Burn hotter and hotter
Where is the broken sword
And the soldier
That stood alone
In a desperate fight
To his heart
She will forever cling

Back Then
We remember
That old screen door
That we had to open
To get inside
Of that old country store
That we used to visit
Time and time again

The song

Mama and Jesus
Made me think
Of the digital video
That I created
Yesterday evening
Titled the True
Wild Wood Flower

Is It

Is it a stone
It is a shell
Is it a mortar
Is it in the wilderness
Is it a sock made
For a big toe
Is it a railroad track
Giving warning
Of the car-roof walker
It is none of them
Because
There is nothing
To the final
End of purpose

Once there was a mule.
Who was too mean for school.
He was always getting caught
breaking all the rules.
Then one day   he came to the LRC.
He soon found it was the place to be.
Who is this mule that we are speaking about
It is John W. Burton, No doubt

Thoughts

The brain's
Thoughts of thinking
Think about the thoughts
That one sentence
Can carry
You may be amazed
To find out
That one thought
Is much better
Than another
Not all thoughts
Are good
To think about

Fire of Love

At last within the church
There was a loud amen
How quickly the seats
Were being filled
With a heavy rattle
In a fighting battle
Our sacred
Fire of love
Has grown
Cold and dead
We had a little stove
To warm this day
25 December 1783

Dreaming

Drifting over
The Blackbird mountain
Sweetly
As a Southern
Spoon
With a plate
And a fork
At the base
Of this mountain
Day break
Travels quickly
When will
The dreaming
Moons shine again
Which
Will prove
That dreams
Are real

No Blackberries From Blackberry Mountain Market

She pushed her
Shopping cart
Down the isle of the
Blackberry Mountain Market
She was at the end
Of her shopping list
The most important
Item that she wanted
Was not there
Blackberries from
Blackberry Mountain
She had to give up
There were no blackberries
Inside of the market
Upon Blackberry Mountain
She went home
There were other
Markets
Upon other mountains
But still there were no
Blackberries anywhere
The Blackberry Mountain
Market became
Quiet and calm that night
Blackberry Pickers from
The Blackberry Mountain
Picked and stocked
Blackberries back
On the shelf inside of
The Blackberry Mountain Market
Why go to any market
That doesn't have
The most important
Item on the shelf
That you want

Reality

Out of the darkness
Shines the bright
Yellow moon
Magic sets the winds
A howling
There is only one
Mortal sky
We all have been soaked
In Kentucky rain
There are many deer
Drinking from
The mountain streams
Many hunters have pursued
They have never
Matched their bullets
Within their dreams
A friend an enemy
To where the words
Went wrong
With her knife was whittled
A different kind of art
How can you be seen
As you really are
You are many miles
Away from the nearest star
You have been seen as one
Light as it falls
From the sun
All day the snow
Fell on Eastern Kentucky
I saw you then
The bird of snow
So from the thousand
Visions out of darkness
I can see the rising sun
Ice crystals became art
The snow storm
Walks upon

The Blackbird Mountain Cliffs
Like hunters
Crying in the snow
The dust loses
Its powers
When the Fire glitters
throughout the night
The winds take
Giants from their
Sacred homes

Being There

As the ages melt away
We all have lived
Throughout labor's
Hurried time
There are many secrets
Within every heart
And mind
In the end
Brighter hopes
Will be there
To find

Alone on the Water

You have traveled
Many days
Upon the water
Troubles you have seen
You care not
For your debts
You have nobody
To travel with
You have every day
For every climb
You care less
For wealth
Than you care
For good health
It is great
That you depend
On friends
Are they proved
To be true
It is better to borrow
Than to own
If a hurricane rises
From a mid-day sky
And the sun
Becomes lost
Never sit down
With tears
In your eyes
Paddle your own canoe

Life's Travels

The storm is high
Above the cliffs
No drops of rain
Will ever be as pleasant
As the mingled
Draught of life
Enjoy your travels
Finding Blackbird Mountain
When you find it
You will learn
The checkered
Flags of life
Your voice will live
In a mellowed
Measurement of peace

Life's Journey of Battles

Where did the bravest
War begin
You will not
Find it on a map
It was a war
Fought by each
Of us
It wasn't fought
By any weapons
Not with any words
Or thoughts
The bravely was silent
In each of our
Own battlefields
The battles
Last so long
From babyhood
To the grave
The battles were
Endless wars
The silence goes down
When a soldier
Is being carried way

Distant Past

It was a mountain
Of sadness
Sweet lingered the songs
Of the wind
Sorrow was born
Every day
The echoes were
Walking like rolling
Marbles
Upon streets of dirt
My thoughts lived up there
Never going anywhere
Some hundred years ago
I walked miles
And miles without
Wearing shoes
On my feet
From the far away
Mountain I could see
A rail road car
I kept walking
And walking
I never made it there
I smiled with tears
In my eyes
During my boyhood years
I treaded along
All of my life
Through the lands
Of the dead
The fire light faded away
Every distant year
I dream and dream
Of the days
That I will see no more
The land she proved
A terrible plague
The river runs

Below with all
Of her force
Life was great
Beneath the green turfs
Where the wild
Flowers bloomed
Don't forget you
Were always alone
In your own world

Today We Part

There is always
A fair harvest
From the age
That has passed
To the age
That waits for you
Wildwood flowers
Are the first flowers
Of the wilderness
To bloom
Stars of the night
Calms the storms
You have been blest
Through many
Of life's tears
You were always
Frightened by all
Of your treasured thoughts
Of friendships and hopes
Let not the moss
Cover the new ground
That you are going to walk
Don't forget that we will
Meet again

The River's Songs

With my hand
On the fiddle strings
I sing the songs
Of the river
As she taught me well
For many days and nights
You came to hear
The music of the river
Coming from my canoe
The downstream
Of the river was far away
I didn't go there
Upon the river bank
My canoe stayed
While a big ship
Was moving slowly
To the river's stream
Far away
My songs and my fiddle
I continued to sing and play
The river's music

Peanut Butter

It was at the end
Of my shopping list
At Wal-Mart today
The most important
Item I did not find
Peanut Butter
Other grocery shoppers
Were looking for it too
That night there was no
Peacte at the dinner table
Because there was no
Peanut Butter

Up There

The field bed
Became the ground
At the time when a king
Reigned beyond the seas
He was a beggar
But wanted to see
What cupid's arrow
Could do
Dogs at night
Barks against the moon
It was the Raven
Not the crow
Which nightly sung
Its song
While resting
In an old apple tree
There I was
Standing tiptoed upon
Blackbird Mountain's cliff
Every minute seemed
To equal many days
The sweet discourses
Of time were born
Don't forget
That the villains
Will always be there
Go looking for them
Find the means
For someday it will
Be yours

Aged Poor and Slow

The man was old
Ragged and gray
He walked slowly
With the chill
Of the winter's day
The ground was covered
Deep with ice and snow
Everyone passed him by
The carriage wheels
And the horse's feet
Coasted past him
Down the slippery street
He was aged
Poor and slow
One day you
Will be just
Like this man
You will become poor
And old and gray
No one will help you
Like for this man
Help will be far away

Dreaming

I dreamed it was
Me shooting marbles
In the sand
All of the players
Were assembled there
If I were to win
I would become
Richer too
For many miles
Away they would
Know my name
I awakened
From my dream
I could not
Remember shooting
Marbles in the sand

Mother's Child

My mother sat there
It was sacred
That old arm chair
She always prayed
While she knelt
Beside that old arm chair
I watched her many days
Her eyes begin to grow dim
And her hair became gray
Year by year rolled on
The last one is here
I saw her die
Sitting in that old arm chair
Today I also have grown old
I don't have any tears

Mother Nature's Song

The endless train
The North-East
Sends its rage
Dusky wreaths
Seem to rise
By swift degrees
The wish of nature
A perfect calm
Throughout
The closing woods
The Mountain seems
Impatient to demand
At last clouds
Shake the dimpled creek
All was mixed
In the wild concert
Within the warbling brooks
Wondering views
Bright enchantments bend
Amusive arches
Before him fly
Living herbs
Profusely wild
Bursts his blinding way
Climbing
To the mountain top
With vision pure
He entered into
The secret stores
A stranger
To the savage
Arts of life
The sluggard
Sleep beneath
A sacred beam
Their light will slumber
And slowly slip away
The thrilling

Exhausted more
A glaring lion
Emerged from
The gloomy woods
Desponding fear
That noble wish
A shoreless ocean
Tumbled around
The earth
There were no storms
No tornadoes with rage
Slept the waters
Relaxing on the
Springs of life

The Voice

The words of Plato
Were never more-worthy
Of a prognostic
Swarm of bees
Than were the voice
Of this Holly Man
Little did I suppose
That in the wild woods
Of Eastern Kentucky
That I would meet
Such a person
When he spoke
My blood ran cold
And my whole frame
Began to shiver
My soul kindled
With the wind
He spoke to me
With his soft voice
Pardon your enemies
Socrates died
As a philosopher
His blindness I recalled
The recollection
Of Old Homer
Standing on a rock
Where you can see
The flood
With the blind eyes
Of a prophets fire
Mother's Kitten Became a Cat
Your mother is the cat
Among her kittens
She reared all
Of her little ones
And she raised
One of them
To become

A strong cat
The nations heard
About him
They led him away
In chains
To a land unknown
The mother cat
Of all of her kittens
Became heart broken
The Opened Book
Sacred feelings
Of the heart
A happy world
Sometimes nature
Shows us
Her careless hand
And her harmful voice
At other times
She shows us
Her whispering breeze
Wonders rise from
This philosophical world
There is always
A trip backwards
Through time
Turn from her eyes
Your fame is fading away
It is the wildwood flowers
That shows us
The colorful blooms
Of life
The time will come
When there will be
A darkened sun
Sprits will be seen
From distances far away
The creeks will be
Full of tears
Don't interrupt
The people's dreams

Of ten thousand fears
With a smile
The yellow topaz burns
While she wears
The robe of Spring
From theme to theme
From horses and hounds
To churches
To politics
To ghosts
The tappers danced
Like rain coming
Down from the stormy sky
Think of nature
As always being

A Little Girl's Morning Prayer

It is early morning
A little girl
Is saying her
Morning prayer
I thank thee
Dear Lord Jesus
For all
Of the animals,
Food
Trees
Water
Flowers
Daddy
And
Mother
I thank thee
For the gifts
Of sharing
So preciously
And the many hours
Of happiness
That I have had
Throughout my childhood
I thank thee
For my
Clothes
Picture Books
And
Toys
Please Lord
Always teach me
To be good to other
Little girls and boys
Lord bless
All of them
Who care for me
Help me to grow
To be happy

And become a helpful
Child
Since I began praying
I have always loved thee

A little Boy's Bed Time Prayer

I thank thee
Heavenly Father
If you would
Help me to put away
All of my wrongs
That I have done today
Make me sorry
True and good
Make mother
And father
Love thee
As much as I do
Lord make me feel
Very happy
Both day and night
You can always
See me Heavenly Father
I know that
You can hear my prayer
Take me
Thy child
Into thy care
Let all of your
Angels
Pure and bright
Watch me and protect
Me throughout the night

Fire Cracker Dan
And His Next OF Kin

Weezer-Sharpest dog on the trail
Bluetick-Dog of Thunder
Calico Cat-Weeper
Fire Cracker Dan
Fire Cracker Nan
Easter Chicken
Memorial Day
Independence Day
Veterans Day
Thanksgiving Turkey
Santa Claus
Santa's Helper the Elf
Christmas Tree
Snowman
Christmas Reindeer
The Kentucky Children's Fix it
Christmas Family
Happy New Year 2020
Valentines Girl
Daniel Boone
Abraham Lincoln
Eastern Kentucky Coal Miner
Richard Hickman Menefee

Fire Cracker Dan

He can dance the dance of a
thousand soldiers dancing in a
marching band and he can do
much more.

Fire Cracker Nan

Investigated The disappearance of Ichabod
Crane.

Easter Chicken

Easter is a Christian festival and cultural
holiday commemorating the resurrection
of Jesus from the dead, described in the
New Testament as having occurred on
the third day of his burial following
his crucifixion by the Romans at
Calvary c. 30 AD.

Memorial Day

A federal holiday in the United
States for mourning the U.S.
military personnel who have died
while serving in the United States
armed forces. It is observed on
the last Monday of May.

Independence Day

A federal holiday in the United States
since 1941, but the tradition of
Independence Day celebrations goes
back to the 18th century and the
American Revolution.

Veterans Day

A federal holiday in the United States
observed annually on November 11,
for honoring military veterans of the
United States Armed Forces.

Thanksgiving Turkey

A national holiday celebrated in late
November each year in the United
States. It began as a day of giving
thanks for the blessing of the harvest
and of the preceding year.

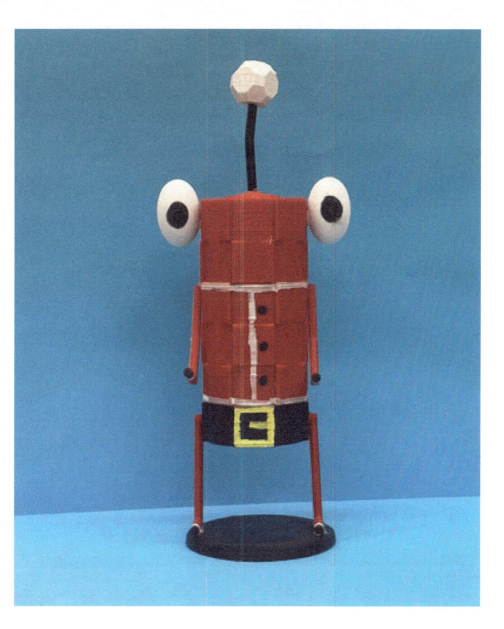

Santa Claus

The original Santa Claus
Was Saint Nicholas
He was a Christian bishop
Who helped the needy
After his death
The legend

Of his gift-giving grew
Saint Nicholas transformed
into the legendary character
We know today
As Santa Claus
Who delivers Christmas presents
To all of the children
Around the world

Santa's Helper the Elf

Christmas Elves tasks
Include making toys
As Christmas gifts
Taking care
Of the reindeer
Baking cookies

Making candy
Preparing Santa's sleigh
And assisting Santa
With other tasks
One of the primary tasks
Of Christmas Elves
Is the making
Of toys all year long
At the Home
Of Santa Claus
The North Pole

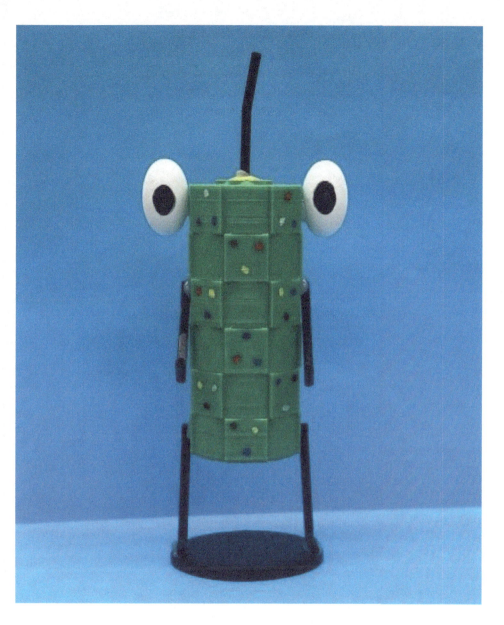

The Christmas Tree

Germany started
The Christmas tree tradition
As we now know it
Sometime in the 16th century
When Christians brought
Decorated trees into their homes

It is believed that Martin Luther
The 16th-century Protestant reformer
Was the first to add lighted candles
to the Christmas Tree

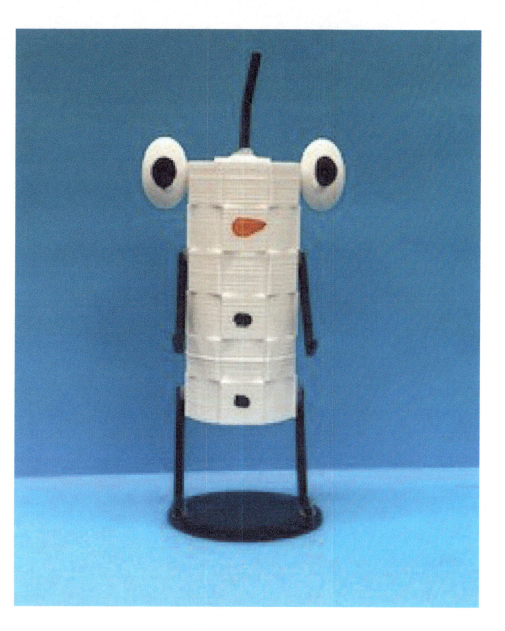

The Snowman

One of the most famous
Christmas animated Television
Christmas specials
Is Frosty the Snowman
It debuted in 1969
Frosty melts

But Santa Claus explains
That Frosty is made
Out of special Christmas snow
And he can never truly melt

The Christmas Reindeer

Santa Claus's Reindeer
Dasher, Dancer, Prancer,
Vixen, Comet, Cupid,
Donner and Blitzen
But there's more to the story
Santa's original eight reindeer

Were first introduced
In A Visit from St. Nicholas
More commonly known today
As The Night Before Christmas

The Kentucky Children
Named him Fix It
Touch one of his colors
And he can fix
Anything that is broken

The Christman Family together ready to celebrate the Christmas Holidays

Happy New Year's Day 2020

A festival observed in most of the world
on 1 January, the first day of the year

The Valentine Girl

Celebrated annually on February 14.

Daniel Boone

Famous for his exploration and
settlement of what is now Kentucky.

Abraham Lincoln

An American lawyer and statesman who served
as the 16th president of the United States.

Easter Kentucky Coal miner

The coal mining industry employed
just over four thousand people in
Kentucky in 2020, of which 75 percent
worked in underground mines.

Richard Hickman Menefee

Menifee County Kentucky was named
after him.

The Blue Stone Ring Tea-Shirt

John Wesley Burton designed this Fire Cracker Dan T-Shirt.
I have had T-Shirts at Amazon.com made in California.
This shirt was made by a retired school teacher and bus
driver working for the Menifee County, Kentucky
Board of Education.

John Wesley Burton was born in Morehead, Kentucky. He presently lives in Pomeroyton, Kentucky bordering Red River Gorge. He is an employee at Morehead State University, and serves as a friend's board member for Kentucky Educational Television (KET), recently receiving the distinguished honor of the 0 Leonard Press award. He holds a Bachelor of Arts Degree and a Master of Arts Degree from the College of Education at Morehead State University.

Elise Claire Cahill was born in Beaufort South Carolina. She presently lives in Lexington Kentucky. She was formerly a student employee at Morehead State University. She holds a Bachelor Business Administration Accounting Area Degree at Morehead State University.

Made in the USA
Monee, IL
19 April 2024

57100914R00095